Introduction

Throughout history dictators have ruled various nations, some brutally and some

benevolently. The United States has often worked with dictators in order to achieve and/or

maintain its national interests. However, the 2002 National Security Strategy argues that

stability, security, and economic vitality can only be achieved through free democratic

governments and free markets.[1] Although, in certain ethnically diverse countries, one can argue

that dictatorship may be the only effective means of governance. This paper seeks to understand

governance of multi-ethnic countries using the former Yugoslavia and Iraq in order to examine

whether or not dictators may be the only effective form of government. The author will compare

and contrast Josip Tito and Saddam Hussein's governments and the tools they utilized to govern

ethnically diverse populations. The paper seeks to understand the context in which war broke

out amongst the populations after the dictators were gone. The comparison of these two dictators

and the outcomes of their removal may lead to a broader understanding of dictator removal and

whether or not it benefits the United States.

Dictatorships: Definition and Types

There are various definitions and forms of dictatorships. Hallgarten defines a dictatorship as

the forcible rule of an individual based on the ruler's alleged position, spurring both laws and

tradition and supported by broad masses which are pushed into action by a social crises or

revolution.[2] Merriam-Webster defines a dictator as, "a person granted absolute emergency

power; one holding complete autocratic control; one ruling absolutely and often oppressively."[3]

A key point of both Hallgarten's and Merriam-Webster's definition is the dictator gains support

and/or takes control by a preceding crises, emergency, or revolution.

Dictatorships take various forms and the basis of which are usually ideologies and/or the

degree of control a dictator exercises. This paper will limit its focus to totalitarian dictatorships because the regimes of Tito and Hussein exerted total control over government and society. The key word for this type of dictatorship is, "total," total control of the people by the state. There is no human activity; political, economic, social, religious, or educational exempt from governmental control.[4] The extent to which the governments of Tito and Hussein fit into these characteristics is discussed later.

Brzezinski and Friedrich identify six characteristics of a totalitarian regime; a total ideology, a single mass party, a terroristic secret police, a monopoly of mass communication, all instruments to wage combat are in the control of the same hands, and a centrally directed planned economy.[5] Brzezinski and Friedrich state that totalitarian dictatorships emerge after the seizure of power by the leaders of a movement who have developed support for an ideology. The point when the government becomes totalitarian is when the leadership uses open and legal violence to maintain its control.[6] The dictator demands unanimous devotion from the people and often uses a real or imaginary enemy to create a threat so the people rally around him.[7] The tools dictators use to manipulate the people are propaganda through mass communication, a single party which reaches every community, an education system that indoctrinates the people, and the use of secret police. However, no matter the amount of propaganda and/or violence a dictator uses, he must provide for the needs of the people to maintain power.

Ethnicity and Conflict

There are no clear rules or standards by which a group of people's identity and/or ethnicity are defined but for consistencies sake, this paper employs Eller's approach for defining ethnic groups. Eller found several words common to many of the definitions of 'ethnic group': symbolism, meaning and identity, cohesion, solidarity, and belonging.[8] He, himself, defines an ethnic group as a social collectively of any nature or antiquity and can successfully claim an identity and rights to be an ethnic group. According to Eller, a key factor is self awareness among the members of the group to define itself using their history (or perceived history) and culture.[9] Eller argues not all ethnic groups are culturally distinct groups, nor are all culturally distinct people part of an ethnic group. People may have the same culture but not necessarily be part of an ethnic group; only when those people identify and organize do they become an ethnic group. This organization and identification is what Eller calls, "ethnic consciousness."

The source of understanding ethnic conflict is to understand how groups organize, interpret, and use their cultures and histories to define themselves and make claims in confrontational and violent ways.[10] Yugoslavia and Iraq are examples of where people became ethnically conscious once their dictators were gone and eventually led to ethnic conflict. Each country experienced ethnic awakenings of various degrees prior to and during each dictator's reign. However, these awakenings were often brutally crushed by the dictator. Further discussion of these ethnic awakenings is discussed later.

Not all Multi-ethnic societies are prone to ethnic violence or unable to democratize, India and Switzerland are examples of stable functioning multi-ethnic democratic states. Two significant factors can, however, serve as predictors of ethnic violence if and when a dictator is removed. When there is a lack of civil society organizations prior to democratization then the likelihood of violence increases.[11] Clubs, unions, and associations are examples of trans-ethnic organizations that can tie people together.[12] The second factor is a lack of a secure environment where all citizens have access to state services.[13] Where a security vacuum exists and limited resources are available then the elites give preference to members of their own ethnic groups.[14] Therefore, cleavages deepen along ethnic lines as those groups compete for security and resources. In turn, when a democratic government is introduced then political parties are formed around the ethnic groups, unlike the U.S. where political parties are defined by an ideology.[15] These conditions existed both in Yugoslavia and Iraq.

Yugoslavia: History and Ethnic Conflict

Yugoslavia, like Iraq, was born after World War I. The Kingdom of Serbs, Croats and Slovenes was established in 1918. It was later renamed Yugoslavia by King Alexander I after he dissolved parliament in January 1929. Following WW I, the Kingdom suffered greatly from a power struggle between the Croats and the Serbs. The Serbians, who were in power, wanted a strong centralized government, while the Croats wanted a decentralized federalist government. This ethnic struggle led to the eventual collapse of the parliament and the establishment of an autocracy by King Alexander I. He was then assassinated in 1934 and succeeded by his cousin, Prince Paul who reigned until World War II. During WW II the majority of the country was governed by Italy, Germany, and Hungary. The most problematic regions; inner Serbia, some of Croatia, and Bosnia-Herzegovina, were placed under the control of the Croatian and radically anti-Serb Ustašas party who had been given sanctuary in Italy by Mussolini prior to WW II. Given absolute power, the Ustašas sought to rid the country of Serbs by executing a plan designed to kill a third, expel a third to Serbia, and convert the remaining third to Catholicism. This killing led to a cycle of massacres and reprisals which continued throughout WW II.

Tito gained his fame during WW II as a partisan fighter who consolidated power and established a communist Yugoslav government following the war.[16] Tito was to establish total control over the country but his communist ideology prevented him from establishing any trans-ethnic organizations. After Tito's death in 1980 the old ethnic struggle between Croatia and Serbia arose again. The communist security apparatus was no longer strong enough to keep Yugoslavia together. The Serbs wanted a strong centralized government in Belgrade and the

Croats wanted total autonomy. The Bosnians found themselves caught in the middle; once the Serbs took an anti-Muslim view it then became a power struggle between three ethnic groups.[17] In 1991 splintering governments attempted to fill the resulting security vacuum. War followed and ended with the Dayton peace accords in 1995. War re-erupted in Kosovo in 1996 and ended with NATO's intervention in 1999. Throughout the former Yugoslavia, peace was only restored through its dissolution into separate ethnically defined countries and the introduction of peace-keeping forces.

Many have argued that Yugoslavia was a nation of differing ethnic groups who never got along and thus splitting up land and population into mono-ethnic states is the only peaceful option. However the people of Yugoslavia share the same Slavic origins and speak the same language (Serbo-Croatian).[18] Prior to an ethnic awakening which began in the mid to late 1800's for the Serbs and Croats, and the mid to late 1980s for the Bosnian Muslims; religion was the only significant difference between the people. During the 1800's as Ottoman influence waned and Austro-Hungarian rose, the Croats and Serbs had an ethnic awakening. This awakening became intertwined with nationalistic goals of independence from the Ottoman and Austro-Hungarian Empires. This nationalism also became aligned with religion, Croats and Slovenes were primarily Roman Catholic, Serbians Eastern Orthodox, and Bosnians primarily Muslim.[19] The Bosnians did not choose to be identified as an ethnic group until they were specifically targeted for their Muslim faith, primarily by the Serbians in the mid-1980s.

Slobodan Milosevic's promotion of Serbian nationalism and vilifying of the Muslims caused his rise to prominence in 1986 and his accession to the presidency in 1989.[20] Therefore this targeting of the Muslims in Bosnia and Kosovo directly led to an ethnic awakening amongst the people. Once war ensued when Croatia and Slovenia declared independence in 1991 the violence became much worse in Bosnia due to Serbia's policy of "ethnic cleansing."

Josip Tito and his Government

Josip Tito was born May 1892 in a small Croatian village as the seventh of fifteen children. His father, Franjo Broz, was a Croat blacksmith who married his mother, Maija, who was a Slovene. Tito's mixed ethnic background likely influenced his future mixed ethnic policies as president. Tito's peasant family was continuously in debt, and he worked on the farm from the age of seven. In 1907 Tito became a machinist's apprentice in city of Sisak. Here he was exposed to the labor movement and joined the Union of Metalworkers and the Social-Democratic Party. Tito spent the next six years working in Slovenia, Bohemia, and Germany. In 1913 he returned to Croatia to fulfill his two-year military obligation. Tito thrived in the Army and emerged as the youngest Sergeant-Major in his regiment. During World War I, he distinguished himself as a soldier, but was captured by the Russians. He learned Russian during his captivity and after being freed by revolting workers in 1917 became involved in the Bolshevik Revolution. After being captured again and escaping he joined the Red Guard and the Communist Party. During this time period Tito met his future wife, Pelagija Belousova, a Russian girl. Tito and his wife returned to Yugoslavia in 1920.[21]

Upon his return to Yugoslavia he joined the Communist Party of Yugoslavia (CPY); his communist activity landed him in prison for five years.[22] Upon his release Tito worked full time for the CPY and began making frequent trips to the Soviet Union.[23] In 1937 Tito had climbed to the top of the CPY which was a difficult feat due to the Stalinist purges taking place in the Soviet Union.[24] World War II gave Tito the opportunity to rise and eventually create a communist Yugoslavia.

After the Axis occupation of Yugoslavia in WW II, Tito and a group of communist partisans began a widespread guerilla campaign against the occupiers. Tito and his partisans also fought a civil war against the anti-communist Chetniks.[25] In 1943 Tito was so successful that his partisans were formally recognized at the Tehran Conference. This led to Allied support with equipment and supplies and, by war's end, Tito had become Yugoslavia's hero and leader. [26]

After WW II, Stalin sought total control of communist countries through the Cominform which was established in 1947.[27] Tito, however, asserted his autonomy and Stalin expelled Yugoslavia from Cominform in 1948. Tito then developed his own brand of communism called, "Titoism." This provided the western powers an opportunity to undermine Soviet influence. Western economic aid began flowing to Tito and his regime.[28] This aid exceeded two billion dollars by 1960 which allowed Yugoslavia to prosper and facilitated the development of Titoism.[29] This split also gave Tito the opportunity to purge his party and government of potential adversaries. More than 11,000 party members were arrested and expelled; another 2,500 were imprisoned on the barren island of Goli Otok, Yugoslavia's version of a gulag.[30]

Tito and his lieutenants believed that the basis of Stalinist communism was wrong. They believed that power should not be concentrated in the state. Instead, they thought power should be placed in the people and the state would wither away. From this new ideology the CPY changed its name to the League of Communists of Yugoslavia (LCY) and implemented Worker's Councils to develop power at the lowest level. Tito maintained tight control of the government, but during the 1960s – 1970s he gave more and more autonomy to the separate republics. A key reason for autonomy was an attempt to revive the economy which was beginning to show weakness. This was mainly due to a centrally controlled planned economy.

Therefore the economy was unable to quickly adapt to consumer needs and introduction of new technologies, but Western aid kept the government afloat.[31]

Prior to Tito's rule, Yugoslavia was a very poor rural country. Under Tito's leadership industrial infrastructure and education and health care systems were established. This combined with infusion of western aid raised Yugoslav's living standards: infant mortality fell, life expectancy increased, literacy increased, and urban populations exploded. Belgrade's population grew from 200,000 to 1.6 million under Tito's reign. Much of the economic wellness was a façade because the centrally controlled economy could not adapt and was propped up by western aid.[32] Additionally, without Tito's leadership the economy became unglued when he died in 1980.

Government propaganda permeated every aspect of Yugoslav life. From the first day of school children were taught to love Tito, Titoism, and Yugoslavia. All education was multi-cultural, discussing each of the differing peoples of Yugoslavia which included trips to adjoining Yugoslav Republics. Tito stressed people could be proud of their origins (Croat, Serb, Muslim-Slav, or other) and also being Yugoslav. Military conscripts did tours outside of their home republic in order to see the different Yugoslav population and region. Key positions in the government bureaucracy were rotated between each republic. Tito's system benefited the more rural and smaller ethnic groups the most. Croat and Serb nationalism was already well established prior to Tito, but under his rule he allowed all groups to thrive culturally and evolve. The seeds of ethnic identity for the Muslim Bosnians were nurtured under Tito.[33]

No amount of propaganda was able to hide the economic hardships Yugoslavia endured during the 1970s and onward. The oil crises of 1973 and 1979 had profound impacts upon

Yugoslavia. Many Yugoslavs were working in Western Europe and this influx of money dried up when unemployment rose throughout Europe during the oil crises.

Tito gave more autonomy to each of the republics in hopes of economic revival. In order to meet the full expectations of Titoism, power distributed to the lowest level, the revised 1974 constitution gave all Yugoslavia's republics sovereignty and independence under a federal government. Foreign affairs, defense and essential economic matters were centrally controlled by the federal government, but decisions had to have the concurrence of the republics. Much of this decentralization led to loss of fiscal control as each of the republics began taking out their own loans without any oversight. Foreign debt rose from 3.5 billion dollars in 1973 to more than 20.5 billion dollars in 1981. Wasteful duplication between the republics also occurred. For example, Slovenia and Montenegro develop expensive sea ports even though one was already established in Croatia and was able to handle all of Yugoslavia's sea trade. Tito attempted to redistribute wealth from the richest republics of Slovenia, Croatia, and Serbia to the poorest; Bosnia-Herzegovina, Macedonia, Montenegro, and Kosovo, but these actions inflamed animosities and sparked nationalism amongst the Croats and Serbs.[34]

Yugoslavia's university system was graduating many students from the urban and rural areas, but student's high expectations of employment only led to discontent when they were not realized. Student protests began to erupt due to the economic conditions, and old animosities between the Serbs and Croats began to manifest themselves in the protests.[35] Everything culminated from 1979 – 1980; the oil crises of 1979, skyrocketing debt, foreign loans and aid dried up, and the death of Josip Tito in 1980. Over the next ten years Yugoslavia experienced a freefall that led to war and the disintegration.

Iraq: History and Ethnic Conflict

Following the aftermath of World War I Great Britain cobbled together Iraq from three Ottoman provinces; Baghdad, Basra, and Mosul.[36] From 1920 till 1968 Iraq experienced the fall of two British imposed monarchies and multiple military coups.[37] Not until Ba'athist seizure of power in 1968 did Iraq achieve a stable form of government. From the Ba'ath movement Saddam Hussein rose to president in July 1979 where he ruthlessly controlled Iraq for almost 24 years.[38] Following the demise of Hussein the security vacuum caused the population to rally around their tribes and religious sects to seek protection. The rallying led to an ethnic consciousness amongst three major ethnic groups; Kurds, Sunnis, and Shiites.[39] This was not the first time an ethnic awakening had occurred amongst the people of Iraq.

Iraq's history is filled with tribal and religious conflict. In 637 Arab Muslims defeated the Persians occupying Iraq, but Islamic conversion and settling Iraq proved difficult for the Arabs.[40] The Arabs did not venture into the northern mountainous region which was settled by the Kurdish people.[41] During the seventh century competing dynasties for the next caliph led to conflict in Karbala, Iraq where the greatest schism in Islam occurred, the division of Sunni and Shiite was created.[42] Iraq and Islam experienced a golden age which lasted until 1258, but the cleavages originating from the Sunni-Shi'a split, and the Arabs and Persians made Iraq vulnerable to the invasion of Genghis Khan.[43] Continued conflict between the Safavid ruler in Iran and Ottoman Turks over Iraq continued to intensify the Sunni-Shia split.[44] It was not until 1638 that Iraq was under Ottoman control.[45] However, the Ottomans could not impose direct control until 1869 due to the continuous tribal conflict amongst the nomadic people of Iraq.[46] Following World War I Iraq was dominated by the British under the mandate system.[47]

Iraq soon proved as difficult for the British to rule as it was for the Ottomans. In 1920 a revolt spread throughout Iraq, foreign rule proved to be a unifying factor of the differing groups of Iraq.[48] The British brutally put down the revolt primarily through the use of the Royal Air Force. The British installed King Faisal to rule Iraq, but to ensure he never became a unifying force the British counterbalanced Faisal by granting land ownership to key sheikhs and local tribal communities.[49] In addition, the majority of the leadership was from the minority Sunnis, therefore the government was dependent upon the British to control the majority Shiites and Kurds. This led to the King of Iraq being unable to control all the tribes from Baghdad, which proved disastrous for the long-term Iraqi political development.[50]

These divisions ensured that broadly based political and civic organizations did not take root. In addition, even if such groups wanted to mobilize, the population of Iraq was only five to ten percent literate.[51] The ability for mass communication and mobilization was limited. Iraq witnessed another British implemented monarchy during World War II after a brief military coup.

The rise of Arab nationalism culminated in Iraq with the execution of the royal family on July 14, 1958.[52] For a ten year period the Iraqi government suffered multiple military coups as various military factions vied for control.[53] After another coup in 1968, the Ba'athists had established its own militia and intelligence organizations which were readily used by Ahmed Hasan al Bakr and Saddam Hussein to conduct a five year purge to ensure their continued control of Iraq.[54] During the 1970s Bakr became more and more detached from governance due to supposed illness. This allowed Saddam Hussein to ascend to presidency in July 1979. Upon seizing power Saddam conducted another purge to rid the government of all potential rivalries,

22 senior party officials were summarily executed.[55] He installed family and tribal members to top posts in the party and government to ensure his control.[56]

Saddam brutally suppressed uprisings by the Shia and Kurds. During 1980, a militant Shi'a group, al-Da'wa, who was supported by Iran, was brutally put down by Saddam.[57] Ninety –six members were executed, including its leader, Ayatollah al-Sadr, and 30,000 Shia were expelled to Iran.[58] In 1982, Iran supported another Iraqi Shi'a group, Supreme Council for Islamic Revolution in Iraq.[59] Again, Saddam brutally executed its members and families though remnants of the organization continued to survive throughout the 1980s.[60] The Kurds suffered the same consequences as the Shi'a when they attempted to assert their autonomy. During the Iran / Iraq war in the 1980s Saddam conducted systematic depopulation of Kurdish areas through the use of conventional and chemical weapons.[61] Following the Gulf War, both Kurds and Shi'a had uprisings brutally put down by Saddam. Even through these ethnic awakenings amongst the Kurds and Shi'a, an eight year war with Iran, and the Gulf War with the U.S. led coalition Saddam retained control and maintained a functioning government.

The following key factors were the seeds of ethnocentrism that were sown prior to Hussein's removal. Iraqis never gained a national identity because the country of Iraq was drawn up arbitrarily by the British which included three distinct ethnic groups; Sunni, Shi'a, and Kurds who were geographically separated. The Kurds occupied the north, the Sunnis in the central and western areas, and the Shiites occupying southern Iraq. Second, the Kurds and the Shiites which represent the majority were dominated by the minority Sunnis throughout Iraq's history, and the Sunnis leaders often resorted to violence to control the other groups. Finally, Iraq has a long history of ethnic and tribal conflict that proved difficult and sometimes impossible for the Ottomans, the British, and Saddam to fully control. Following the demise of Hussein and the security vacuum that followed, these groups rallied around their ethnic groups for security and resources. At this point the Iraqi people developed political parties that mirrored their ethnic groups. Following the five year elections, the Iraqi government became ethnically aligned. This has led to much corruption because many of the elites are obligated to ensure their group receives limited state resources at the expense of others.[62] Looking through the aforementioned lens, it is difficult to understand why the U.S. administration miscalculated the potential for level of ethnic violence that developed following the toppling of Hussein.

Saddam Hussein and his Government

Saddam Hussein was born April 28, 1937 in the town of Al-Awja. His father Hussein died before he was born. Saddam's mother Sabha could not support him, she sent him to be raised by his uncle, Khairallah Talfah until he was three. His uncle, an army officer and a staunch Arab nationalist, participated in a failed uprising against the monarchy and was arrested and sentenced to five years in prison. During his uncle's incarceration Saddam returned to his mother living in al-Shawish, who remarried a brother of his late father. His uncle's incarceration had a profound impact upon Saddam and was likely the foundations of hate towards the monarchy and spark of Arab nationalism within Saddam. At the age of ten Saddam returned to his uncle in Tikrit after enduring much hardship, cruelty, and no education from his Step-Father. His uncle ensured Saddam was educated and took him to Baghdad in 1955 to live and attend school. Kahairallah's son, three years junior to Saddam, became Saddam's best friend and would later serve as Saddam's defense minister. During this time period Saddam witnessed Arab nationalism sweep the streets of Baghdad. Saddam applied to the Baghdad Military Academy, but failed the entrance examinations.[63]

Saddam joined the Ba'ath party and his first assignment included rallying students and oppressing political opponents with an organized gang in the Baghdad suburb of Karkh. In 1958 Saddam was charged with murder of a government official but was released in six months due to insufficient evidence. As a result of this notoriety, he was given another mission to assassinat Iraq's ruler, General Abd al-Karim Qassem. He only wounded Qassem, who then conducted a purge of the Ba'athists and made Saddam Iraq's most wanted man. Saddam escaped to Syria and then to Egypt. The assassination attempt would later serve as propaganda for Saddam's image. Saddam spent three years in Egypt where he completed his high school and enrolled in law school at the University of Cairo, which he never completed. In Egypt Saddam admired Nasser and witnessed how Nasser established a single party system with a semblance of democracy with his formation of the National Assembly. In 1963 Saddam returned to Iraq after the Ba'ath Party when its Ba'ath militia overthrew Qassem. Upon his return Saddam married his cousin, Sajidah Talfah.[64]

Saddam arrived in Iraq after the Ba'athists had already seized power, thus Saddam was given a minor position in the government. This did not stop Saddam from building a power base and aligning himself with a faction of the Party led by Brigadier Ahmad Hasan al-Bakr, who was the Prime Minister of Iraq and a blood relative of Saddam. The Ba'ath party and the Iraqi government spent much of 1963-1968 in turmoil, and Saddam ended up in prison as the result of a government purge. Saddam later escaped and became Bakr's number two. In 1966 Saddam orchestrated the Extraordinary Regional Congress which led to the split of the Iraqi Ba'ath party from the Syrian Ba'ath party. After the humiliating Arab defeat in the Six Day War, Bakr and Saddam seized power in 1968, "July Revolution." Over the next five years Saddam, as head of the security services, expertly executed a purge of all opponents and potential contenders for power.[65]

In March, 1970 Saddam was instrumental in bringing a peaceful resolution with the Kurds who had been conducting a quasi civil war. He reneged on the original agreement with the Kurds in 1974, and by March, 1974 the Kurdish rebellion had reassumed with Iran's support. Saddam was able to apply pressure against the Kurds through the Soviet Union by signing a bilateral Treaty of Friendship and Cooperation on April 9th, 1972. Additionally, this treaty allowed Iraq to quickly build its military strength to buttress Iranian threats. Saddam also asserted Iraq's authority by nationalizing oil production, until 1972 a consortium of Western countries owned Iraq's oil production. One year later Saddam conceded territory and navigation rights in the Shatt al-Arab to Iran in order to end the bloody rebellion which had cost Iraq 60,000 casualties and an estimated four billion dollars. Within two weeks of the Algiers Agreement with Iran, Saddam effectively suppressed the Kurdish rebellion.[66] This five year period shows Saddam's pragmatic approach and flexibility to successfully confront crises thereby ensuring his political survival.[67]

After purging potential rivals and ending the Kurdish and Iranian crises, Saddam began to solidify his position with the people. He sought to implement social reforms which included a partially controlled economy (primarily oil), universal education, free health care, and emancipation of women. The emancipation of women included enacting legislation that ensured equal pay, protection from job discrimination, and a woman's choice to marry and divorce. Additionally, women were allowed to serve in the military. Ba'athist socialism suffered from inefficiency, waste, and corruption. However, oil revenue ensured economic prosperity despite the problems inherent with Ba'athist socialism. By the late 70s Iraq had established trade relations with many Western powers at the expense of the Soviet Union. Iraq's economic transactions declined to only five percent of its overall trade. Although the Soviet Union remained Iraq's main arms supplier, its share of arms sells dropped from 95 percent in 1972 to 63 percent in 1979. France became Iraq's number two arms supplier. Fearing a Soviet led coup, Saddam purged all communists within the Iraq. On July 16, 1979 President Bakr retired expressing health concerns, thereby allowing Saddam to assume the role of President.[68]

Within two weeks of ascending to the presidency, Saddam again purged the government through another supposed coup. This purge was the larger and deadlier than all previous ones. To further consolidate his power Saddam reorganized his cabinet at the expense of weakening the Revolutionary Command Council (RCC). The RCC previously chose and selected the president, but it no longer had that power after Saddam's purges and reorganization. A symbolic act of democratic reform was the reestablishment of the National Assembly (much like Nasser). The 250 seat assembly was an elected body by the Iraqi citizens. The rules for candidates ensured only Baath's were elected, and the security service ensured only those loyal to Saddam were elected. The Assembly was a vehicle established to propagandize Saddam's embodiment of both the Iraqi state and the Iraqi people who "freely" elected a body loyal to Saddam.[69]

Images of Saddam appeared throughout Iraq, and his presence was inserted into every media outlet and the education system. Saddam televised his continual visits throughout Iraq and his meetings with common Iraqis. One of his popular routines was to disguise himself and visit families to discuss the issues of common people and Iraqi government.[70] Saddam utilized Iraq's ancient history to build an ethnic identity, he harkened back to ancient Mesopotamia, King Nebuchadnezzar, and ancient Babylon.[71] These ancient symbols and the rebuilding of Babylon served as a supposed source of Iraqi pride, identification, and the superiority of Iraqi civilization as the birthplace of civilization. Saddam carefully created a cult of personality that would go unquestioned despite leading Iraq into war with Iran and then two wars with the United States

Iraq fought an eight year war with Iran, 1980-1988, that achieved no territorial gains and cost an estimated 200,000 Iraqi killed and 500,000 wounded.[72] However, Iraq emerged from the war with the region's most powerful armed forces and one of the world's largest Armies. The Iraqi economy enjoyed unprecedented prosperity; oil exports rose from one billion dollars in 1972 to 21 billion dollars in 1979 and 26 billion dollars in 1980.[73] During the war Saddam's liberalization of the Iraqi economy ensured food and supplies were readily available for the population despite the continuing war.[74] Despite the war, many experts agreed that Saddam emerged from the war more powerful (primarily military), more united, and much more of a nation-state.[75] However, Iraq's economic underpinnings remained weak. Dependent upon only one commodity (oil) and stressed by Saddam's grand social and military schemes, the economy would fail without securing vitally needed financial resources. Saddam soon tested his people's patience launching another war in 1990 with Kuwait that led to the eventual war with a U.S. led coalition.

Saddam easily conquered Kuwait in 1990, but was dismayed at the international outrage. Saddam's view was the invasion of Kuwait was necessary; his political future depended on the vital oil resources that Kuwait held. Iraq required oil revenues to support its economy and to pay off over 80 billion dollars in foreign debt accumulated during the Iran / Iraq war.[76] On July 16 in a letter to the Secretary-General of the Arab League, the Iraqi Foreign Minister, Tariq Aziz, accused Kuwait and UAE of a scheme to glut the oil market that exceeded the quotas established by OPEC.[77] This influx of oil caused the price of oil to plummet at the expense of the Iraqi economy. However, Saddam miscalculated the international response and suffered dearly.

17

Iraq's devastating military defeat by the coalition forces in 1991 led to over 12 years of stringent economic sanctions that destroyed Iraq from the inside out.[78] However, Saddam survived and most of the troops destroyed by the coalition forces were poorly trained, badly equipped Shi'a and Kurdish conscripts. Saddam's Republican Guard emerged largely unscathed from the conflict. The Republican Guard guaranteed regime survival when the Kurdish north and Shi'a south simultaneously rose up. The Kurdish and Shi'a uprisings solidified Sunni support for the regime, which led to the systematic crushing of the insurrection.[79] The crushing of their ethnic rebellions and the consolidation of the Sunni regime served as precursors to the ethnic strife that would follow Saddam's demise in 2003.

The UN sanctions and Saddam's refusal to accept the "oil-for-food" deal caused the Iraqi population to spiral into the depths of poverty. However, in spite of the poor circumstances of the Iraqi people, they supported the regime because they were preoccupied with the daily business of survival and thus unable to pose a serious collective challenge to it.[80] In addition, Saddam's systematic control of food distribution was an effective tool to control those that were perceived threats.[81] By 1996, after two failed CIA backed coup attempts and amongst growing unrest, Saddam accepted the "food-for-oil" program.[82] This influx of money and food ensured Saddam's survival.

In 2001 the new Bush administration were many voices advocating more active approaches to dealing with rogue nations, especially Iraq. The events of September 11, 2001 gave the administration an opportunity to seek Iraqi regime change. Operation Iraqi Freedom began in 2003 with the removal of Saddam's regime and continues to the present. The U.S. continues to struggle to establish a safe, secure, and stable Iraq. The U.S. goal to establish a liberal free democracy in Iraq has given way to establishing a stable government due to prolonged conflict and regional instability. Much of the conflict stems from ethnic tensions between the Kurds, Sunnis, and Shiites. Added to the conflict are criminal activities and Al Qaeda stoking the ethnic conflict.

In February 2007 the National Intelligence Estimate reported that, "Civil war accurately describes key aspects of the conflict," but the report acknowledged that there is more than just a civil war at hand.[83] The Fund for Peace failed state index for 2007 rates Iraq second only to Sudan.[84] However, the troop surge beginning in early 2007 has decreased the number of attacks significantly. Department of Defense report to congress in March 2008 state U.S. military force losses are down 72 percent since the May 2007 high, and Iraqi forces' deaths have fallen over 70 percent.[85] The future of Iraq is to be determined, but the likelihood of continued ethnic conflict is high unless U.S. forces remain in large numbers to maintain security. Only through the presence of increased force has ethnic conflict lessened.

Lessons Learned from Tito's and Hussein's Dictatorships

Both the Tito and Hussein regimes show how dictatorships can maintain power and stability in multi-ethnic countries with histories of ethnic conflict. A unified Yugoslavia now exists only in our history books; while the newly installed democracy in Iraq has yet to stand the test of time. However, their exercise of power often violated human rights, led to economic woes and, in Saddam's case, helped cause major regional instability.

Both Yugoslavia and Iraq only experienced prolonged stable governance under dictators, all other types of government failed. Both dictators attempted to instill national identities using their education systems, media outlets, and their own cults of personality. Much of their national identities were drawn from legends and histories of their regions and peoples. However, these identities did not stick. Both dictators suppressed ethnic strife, but once they were gone, their countries fell into ethnic conflict. Sustaining a national identity without the dictators' enforcement proved to be nil. Only through a combination of force, meeting economic needs, and some inclusion in the government could the dictators achieve a sense of nationalism. However, when economic needs were not meet and/or disenfranchisement from the political system, ethnic cleavages appeared. Without dictators these cleavages exploded into ethnic conflict.

Conflict is likely in dictatorships because the passing of authority is always ripe for exploitation. In countries with a history of ethnic conflict, violence is assured if there is no transition to a strong security apparatus that can prevent it. A strong security apparatus can be provided by another dictator or a foreign military presence. Because in Iraq and Yugoslavia there was no transition to a strong security apparatus, much bloodshed ensued.

Conclusion

Advocating or actively supporting dictatorships should not be our nation's normal course of action; however it should remain a possibility if it is the most effective way to keep certain ethnically diverse nations stable. Dictatorships do not necessarily have to be brutally totalitarian; Tito did not employ many of the brutal measures that Saddam used in Iraq. Should the U.S. intercede in a conflict or conduct regime change in the future, but only be willing to accept liberal democracy as form of government, then it must either prepare for a potentially long bloody ethnic conflict or provide security forces robust enough to prevent the outbreak and/or continuation of violence.

Therefore the U.S. should consider the following prior to such interventions. First, regime change should only take place if it is an immediate threat to the U.S., its allies, and/or regional/world stability. Second, if intervention is chosen, thorough analysis of the country's history, culture, and ethnic make-up must be conducted. If the potential for ethnic conflict exists, then the U.S. should consider installing various forms of government and if the country can continue to exist in its current boundaries. Perhaps the country should be split along ethnic boundaries, organized as a loose federation with autonomous regions, or have an autocratic government or benevolent dictatorship installed. Liberal democracy need not be the only form of acceptable government.

Yugoslavia only existed as a nation when controlled by a dictator, it could not have otherwise. Peace was only achieved in the former Yugoslavia through a combination of splitting up, robust security forces, economic and government aid, and much bloodshed. It is too early to see whether or not Iraq will follow the same steps as Yugoslavia. However Iraq, like Yugoslavia, only achieved a stable government under a dictatorship. Iraq's current democracy is held up by massive U.S. support, only time will tell if Iraq will continue as a democracy, revert back to a form of dictatorship, or splinter apart along ethnic lines. Regardless of the outcome, regime change in Iraq will always be questioned if it was worth the monetary and human cost.

Finally, dictatorships may be the only effective means of governing some ethnically diverse countries. Only through careful study of a country's history, culture, and ethnic make-up can a determination be made of the country's governmental system. Yugoslavia and Iraq provide warnings about the possible outcomes of dictator removal. Free democratic regimes must be the preferred forms of government; however they should not be the only acceptable ones. Support for dictatorships should remain in our diplomatic toolbox. Otherwise, the U.S. must accept potential bloodshed, instability (internal and regional), and huge economic costs.

Works Cited

1. White House. *The National Security Strategy of the United States of America* (Washington, D.C.: GPO, 2002), vi.

2. George W. F. Hallgarten, *Why dictators?: The causes and forms of tyrannical rule since 600 B.C.* (London: Macmillan, 1954), 3-4.

3. Merriam-Webster Online Dictionary, <http://www.m-w.com/dictionary/dictator> (13 January 2008).

4. William Ebenstein, *Totalitarianism: New perspectives* (Austin: Holt, Rinehart And Winston, 1962), 5-6.

5. Zbigniew K. Brzezinski, and Carl J. Friedrich, *Totalitarian Dictatorship & Autocracy* (London: Frederick A Praeger), 1968. 294

6. Ibid.

7. Ibid, 57.

8. Jack David Eller, *From Culture to Ethnicity to Conflict: An Anthropological Perspective on Ethnic Conflict* (Ann Arbor: University of Michigan Press, 1999), 12-13.

9. Ibid, 7-11.

10. Ibid, 47.

11. Andreas Wimmer, "Democracy and Ethno-religious Conflict in Iraq." *Survival* 45 (2003): 111-133.

12. Ibid.

13. Ibid.

14. Ibid.

15. Ibid, 120.

16. Christopher Bennett, *Yugoslavia's Bloody Collapse: Causes, Course and Consequence.* (London: NYU Press, 1997), 33-50.

17. Eller, 292-295.

18. Ibid, 245.

19. Ibid, 259-260.

20. Ibid, 288-289.

21. Richard West, *Tito and the Rise and Fall of Yugoslavia: And the Rise and Fall of Yugoslavia.* (New York: Carroll & Graf Publishers, 1994), 24-45.

22. Bennett, 57.

23. Bennett, 57.

24. Ibid.

25. J. A. S. Grenville, *A History of the World in the Twentieth Century.* (Cambridge: Belknap Press, 1994), 287.

26. West, 176.

27. Grenville, 385.

28. Bennett, 59.

29. Ibid.

30. Ibid.

31. Ibid, 59-61.

32. Ibid, 61-66.

33. Ibid, 60-72.

34. Ibid, 61-79.

35. Ibid, 69, 73-74.

36. Andrea J. Dew, and Richard H. Schultz, *Insurgents, Terrorists, and Militias: The Warriors of Contemporary Combat.* (Columbia: Columbia University Press, 2006), 213.

37. Ibid, 214 – 217.

38. Ibid, 216-217.

39. Gawdat Bahgat, "Saddam Hussein's Legacy: A Preliminary Assessment and Future Implications." *SAIS Review* 25 (2005): 95-96.

40. Dew and Shultz, 200-201.

41. Albert Hourani, *A History of the Arab Peoples*. (Cambridge: Belknap Harvard, 1991), 92, 97.

42. Ibid; 31, 36-37.

43. Dew and Schultz, 201-202.

44. Ibid, 202.

45. Hourani, 215.

46. Dew and Schultz, 202.

47. Toby Dodge, *Inventing Iraq: The Failure Of Nation Building And A History Denied*. (Columbia: Columbia University Press, 2005.), 1.

48. Dew and Schultz, 213.

49. Ibid, 213.

50. Ibid, 213.

51. Wimmer, 111-133.

52. Hourani, 409.

53. Dew and Schultz, 216.

54. Ibid, 217-218.

55. Ibid, 218.

56. Ibid, 218.

57. Liam Anderson, and Gareth Stansfield, *The Future of Iraq, Updated Edition: Dictatorship, Democracy, or Division?*. (New York: Palgrave Macmillan, 2005), 126-127.

58. Ibid.

59. Ibid, 127-128.

60. Ibid.

61. Ibid, 170.

62. Wimmer, 113-120.

63. Efraim Karsh, and Inari Rautsi. *Saddam Hussein: A Political Biography*. Washington, (D.C.: Potomac Books, 1991), 1-15.

64. Ibid, 17-21.

65. Ibid, 25-45.

66. Ibid, 84.

67. Ibid, 72-74.

68. Ibid, 86-109.

69. Ibid, 121.

70. Ibid, 122.

71. David B. Des Roches, "Saddam Hussein and the Uses of Political Power" (M.A. diss., University of London, 1990), 11.

72. Anderson and Stansfield, 62.

73. Karsh and Rautsi, 136.

74. Ibid, 196-197.

75. Simon Henderson, *Instant Empire: Saddam Husseins Ambition for Iraq*. San Francisco: (Mercury House, 1991), 115.

76. Karsh and Rautsi, 202.

77. Ibid, 211.

78. Anderson and Stansfield, 83.

79. Ibid, 89

80. Ibid, 93.

81. Ibid.

82. Ibid, 97.

83. Jonathan Karl. "Quick Highlights of the National Intelligence Estimate Report." ABC News: Online news, breaking news, feature stories and more. <http://abcnews.go.com/Politics/story?id=2844849> (accessed March 30, 2008).

84. "Foreign Policy: The Failed States Index 2007." Foreign Policy: Your portal to global politics, economics, and ideas. http://www.foreignpolicy.com/story/cms.php?story_id=3865 (accessed March 30, 2008).

85. Department of Defense. *Measuring Stability and Security in Iraq Report to Congress.* March 2008. < http://www.defenselink.mil/pubs/pdfs/Master%20%20Mar08%20-%20final%20signed.pdf> (30 March 2008), 17.

Bibliography

Anderson, Liam, and Gareth Stansfield. *The Future of Iraq, Updated Edition: Dictatorship, Democracy, or Division?*. New York: Palgrave Macmillan, 2005.

Bahgat, Gawdat. "Saddam Hussein's Legacy: A Preliminary Assessment and Future Implications." *SAIS Review* 25 (2005): 93-103.

Bennett, Christopher. *Yugoslavia's Bloody Collapse: Causes, Course and Consequences*. London: NYU Press, 1997.

Bolton, John R.. "Bring Back the Laxalt Doctrine." *Policy Review* 102 (2000): 3-15.

Brooks, Robin, and Steven Fish. "Does Diversity Hurt Democracy?." *Journal of Democracy* 15 (2004): 154-166.

Brzezinski, Zbigniew K., and Carl J. Friedrich. *Totalitarian Dictatorship & Autocracy*. London: Frederick A Praeger, 1968.

Dew, Andrea J., and Richard H. Shultz. *Insurgents, Terrorists, and Militias: The Warriors of Contemporary Combat*. Columbia: Columbia University Press, 2006.

Des Roches, David B. "Saddam Hussein and the Uses of Political Power," M.A. diss., University of London, 1990.

Carothers, Thomas. "From Victory to Success: Why Dictators Aren't Dominoes." Foreign Policy. July 2003. < http://www.foreignpolicy.com/story/cms.php?story_id=90> (27 January 2008).

Craddock, John, and Barbara R. Fick. "The Americas in the 21st Century The Challange of Governance and Security." *joint forces quarterly* 3rd Quarter (2006): 10-15.

Department of Defense. *Measuring Stability and Security in Iraq Report to Congress*. March 2008. < http://www.defenselink.mil/pubs/pdfs/Master%20%20Mar08%20-%20final%20signed.pdf> (30 March 2008).

Des Roches, David B. "Saddam Hussein and the Uses of Political Power." Masters, diss., University of London, 1990.

Dodge, Toby. *Inventing Iraq: The Failure Of Nation Building And A History Denied*. Columbia: Columbia University Press, 2005.

Ebenstein, William. *Totalitarianism: New perspectives*. Austin: Holt, Rinehart And Winston, 1962.

Eland, Ivan. "What Should the United States do About Saddam Hussein?" Emory Law Journal 50, no. 3 (2001): 833-852.

Eller, Jack David. *From Culture to Ethnicity to Conflict: An Anthropological Perspective on Ethnic Conflict.* Ann Arbor: University of Michigan Press, 1999.

Enloe, Cynthia H. *Ethnic Conflict & Political Development an analytic study.* Toronto: Little Brown & Company, 1973.

Encarnacion, Omar G. "The Strange Persistence of Latin American Democracy." *World Policy Journal* 20, no. 4 (2003): 30-40.

"Foreign Policy: The Failed States Index 2007." Foreign Policy: Your portal to global politics, economics, and ideas. http://www.foreignpolicy.com/story/cms.php?story_id=3865 (accessed March 30, 2008).

Ghalioun, Burhan. "The Persistence of Arab Authoritarianism." *Journal of Democracy* 15, no. 4 (2004): 126-132.

Goldsmith, Arthur A. "Muslim Exceptionalism? Measuring the Democracy Gap." *Middle East Policy* 14, no. 3 (2007): 86-96.

Grenville, J. A. S.. *A History of the World in the Twentieth Century.* Cambridge: Belknap Press, 1994.

Groth, Alexander. "Democratizing the Middle East: A Conservative Perspective?." *Journal of Libertarian Studies* 19 (2005): 3-17.

Hallgarten, George W. F. *Why dictators?: The causes and forms of tyrannical rule since 600 B.C.* London: Macmillan, 1954.

Henderson, Simon. *Instant Empire: Saddam Husseins Ambition for Iraq.* San Francisco: Mercury House, 1991.

Hourani, Albert. *A History of the Arab Peoples.* Cambridge: Belknap Harvard, 1991.

Karl, Jonathan. "Quick Highlights of the National Intelligence Estimate Report." ABC News: Online news, breaking news, feature stories and more. http://abcnews.go.com/Politics/story?id=2844849 (accessed March 30, 2008).

Karsh, Efraim, and Inari Rautsi. *Saddam Hussein: A Political Biography.* Washington, D.C.: Potomac Books, 1991.

Khadduri, Majid. *Socialist Iraq: A study in Iraqi politics since 1968.* Washington D.C.: Middle East Institute, 1978.

Maslow, A.H. "A Theory of Human Motivation." *Psychological Review* 50 (1943): 370-396.

Makiya, Kanan. *Republic of Fear: The Politics of Modern Iraq, Updated Edition.* Berkeley: University of California Press, 1998.

Mihajlov, Mihajlo. "Perspectives: Why Bosnia is noat a Quagmire." The New Leader 75, no. 10 (1992): 5.

Payne, James L. "Does Nation Building Work?" The Independent Review 10 (2006): 597-608.

Puddington, Arch. "Freedomhouse.org: Map of Freedom in the World." freedomhouse.org: Home. http://www.freedomhouse.org/template.cfm?page=363&year=2007 (accessed January 2, 2008).

Radnitz, Scott. "The Tyranny of Small Differences: The Relationship Between Ethnic Diversity and Democracy in the Former Socialist Bloc." *Demokratizatsiya* 12 (2004): 575-606.

Takeyh, Ray. "Close, But No Democracy." *The National Interest* 78 (2004): 57-65.

Vuckovic, Gojko. "Promoting Peace and Democracy in the Aftermath of the Balkan Wars." *World Affairs* 162, no. 1 (1999): 3-10.

West, Richard. *Tito and the Rise and Fall of Yugoslavia: And the Rise and Fall of Yugoslavia..* New York: Carroll & Graf Publishers, 1994.

White House. *The National Security Strategy of the United States of America.* Washington, D.C.: GPO, 2002, vi.

Wimmer, Andreas. "Democracy and Ethno-religious Conflict in Iraq." *Survival* 45 (2003): 111-133.

www.ingramcontent.com/pod-product-compliance
Lightning Source LLC
Chambersburg PA
CBHW081544280526
45788CB00010B/3352